Things That Live on You

George Ivanoff

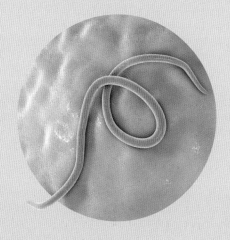

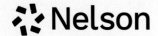

Things That Live on You

Text: George Ivanoff
Publishers: Tania Mazzeo and Eliza Webb
Series consultant: Amanda Sutera
  Hands on Heads Consulting
Editor: Laken Ballinger
Project editor: Annabel Smith
Designer: Leigh Ashforth
Project designer: Danielle Maccarone
Illustrations: Amanda Shufflebotham
Permissions researcher: Debbie Gallagher
Production controller: Renee Tome

Acknowledgements
We would like to thank the following for permission to reproduce
copyright material:

Front cover: Shutterstock.com/Image Source Trading Ltd; front cover,
pp. 3, 9, back cover (top): Shutterstock.com/ChWeiss; pp. 1, 5
(bottom left), 18, back cover (bottom): Alamy Stock Photo/Science Photo
Library/Kateryna Kon; p. 4: Shutterstock.com/Monkey Business Images;
pp. 5 (top), 6: Gilles San Martin/creativecommons.org/licenses/by-sa/2.0/;
p. 5 (middle): Alamy Stock Photo/Science Photo Library/SCIEPRO;
p. 7 (top): Getty Images/Eric Audras, (bottom): Science Photo Library/
Steve Gschmeissner; p. 10: Science Photo Library/Power And Syred;
p. 11 (top): iStock.com/beyhanyazar, (bottom): iStock.com/GlobalP;
pp. 12, 23: Alamy Stock Photo/Science Picture Co; p. 13 (top left): iStock.
com/hirun, (top right): Getty Images/BananaStock, (bottom): iStock.com/
Bet_Noire; p. 14 (top): Science Photo Library/David Mccarthy,
(bottom): iStock/romiri; p. 15 (top): Shutterstock.com/Dmytro Zinkevych,
(bottom): Shutterstock.com/Alex Vog; p. 16 (top right): iStock.com/Sinhyu,
(bottom left): Shutterstock.com/Arie v.d. Wolde; p. 17 (top): iStock.com/
Mypurgatoryyears, (bottom): Shutterstock.com/Ground Picture;
p. 19 (top right): Shutterstock.com/Sorapop Udomsri, (middle left): Alamy
Stock Photo/BSIP/Cavallini James, (bottom right): Shutterstock.com/Irelee;
p. 20: iStock.com/panom; p. 21 (top left): Alamy Stock Photo/Minden Pictures/
Thomas Marent, (top right): Shutterstock.com/Inna Horosheva,
(bottom): Alamy Stock Photo/Iuliia Kuzenkova; p. 22: iStock.com/Monkey
Business Images.

Every effort has been made to trace and acknowledge copyright.
However, if any infringement has occurred, the publishers tender their
apologies and invite the copyright holders to contact them.

NovaStar

Text © 2024 Cengage Learning Australia Pty Limited
Illustrations © 2024 Cengage Learning Australia Pty Limited

ISBN 978 0 17 033416 7

Cengage Learning Australia
Level 5, 80 Dorcas Street
Southbank VIC 3006 Australia
Phone: 1300 790 853
Email: aust.nelsonprimary@cengage.com

For learning solutions, visit **cengage.com.au**

Printed in China by 1010 Printing International Ltd
1 2 3 4 5 6 7 28 27 26 25 24

*Nelson acknowledges the Traditional Owners and Custodians
of the lands of all First Nations Peoples. We pay respect
to Elders past and present, and extend that respect to
all First Nations Peoples today.*

Contents

Your Body Is a Habitat!

The human body is a living thing. But did you know that your body is also a **habitat** for many tiny living creatures?

Everyone you meet has tiny creatures living on them!

There are some creatures you can see, such as head lice in your hair. Some are much too small to see without a microscope, such as eyelash mites. Some are helpful to our bodies, making them work better. Some are harmless, but some can be harmful.

Read on to find out about some of the creatures that can live on you!

Head lice can be seen in the hair on your head.

Eyelash mites can only be seen through a microscope.

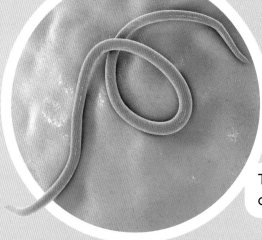

Threadworms are tiny and harmless.

Head Lice

Head lice are small insects that can live in your hair. They can't fly, as they don't have any wings, and they can't jump. But they can run very fast, so they usually spread to new people from head-to-head contact.

Head lice feed on blood. They bite your **scalp** and suck out a small amount of blood. This is why head lice make your head itch.

Scientific name:
Pediculus humanus capitis

Common name: Head lice

Length: About 2.4–3 mm

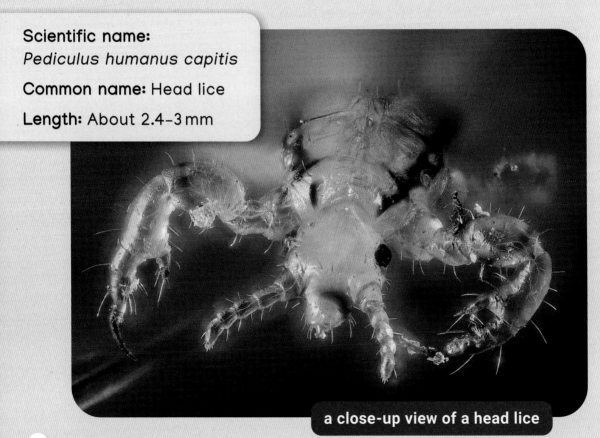

a close-up view of a head lice

Head lice are not harmful, but they can be annoying. You can get rid of them with special shampoo.

If you don't get rid of head lice straightaway, they can live up to 33 days. During that time, they can lay sticky eggs called "nits" that attach to **strands** of your hair. Nits are much harder to get rid of than lice. You have to carefully brush all of them out with a fine-tooth comb.

You need to use a special comb to get nits out of your hair.

Claws

Head lice have hook–like claws that make it easy for them to hold onto a strand of hair. But these claws also make it difficult for head lice to move along other surfaces. If they are brushed off someone's head, it's hard for them to get onto a new head.

Under a microscope, you can see how head lice use their claws to hold onto strands of hair.

Head Lice Life Cycle

The life cycle of head lice lasts for around 33 days.

1
Female lice can lay up to 10 nits a day. The nits are attached to strands of hair.

5
Lice die about 33 days after hatching. But female lice often lay more nits before they die.

4
After 10 days, the lice are fully grown adults and are now ready to lay nits.

2

After 7 days, the nits hatch.
Young lice, or lice that are not
fully grown, are called "nymphs".

3

The nymphs shed their skin
(or lose their outer skin layer)
three times as they grow.

Eyelash Mites

Eyelash mites are **microscopic** creatures that mostly live on your eyelashes and eyebrows. They can also spread to other parts of your face, and even to other parts of your body.

Most people have at least some eyelash mites living on them. But as you get older, you can get more because the eyelash mites lay lots of eggs. Just how many eyelash mites you have is unknown – but it could be thousands!

Scientific name: *Demodex*

Common name: Eyelash mite

Length: About 0.15–0.4 mm

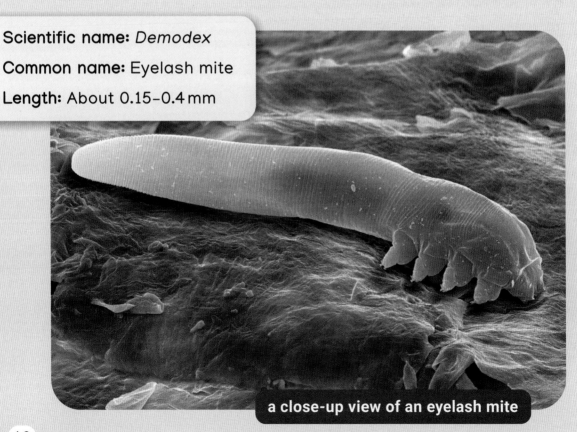

a close-up view of an eyelash mite

Eyelash mites are usually harmless, as long as you don't have too many of them. If you get a lot, it's called an **infestation**. This can result in itching around the eyes or having weak eyelashes that break and fall out. An infestation can be treated with a special cream, spray or wipe.

Most eyelash mites are found on your eyelashes and on the little hairs in your eyebrows.

Arachnids

Eyelash mites are arachnids – small creatures with four pairs of legs and a body divided into two parts. Spiders and scorpions are also arachnids.

four pairs of legs

body divided into two parts

Human Itch Mites

Human itch mites are microscopic creatures that can burrow into the upper layer of your skin. They can then live there, under your skin, eating skin **cells** and laying eggs.

You can get these mites from bedding or towels that have been used by people who have mites. You can also get human itch mites by touching someone who has them on their skin. Mites can spread further across your body when you scratch.

Scientific name:
Sarcoptes scabiei

Common name:
Human itch mite

Length: 0.2–0.35 mm

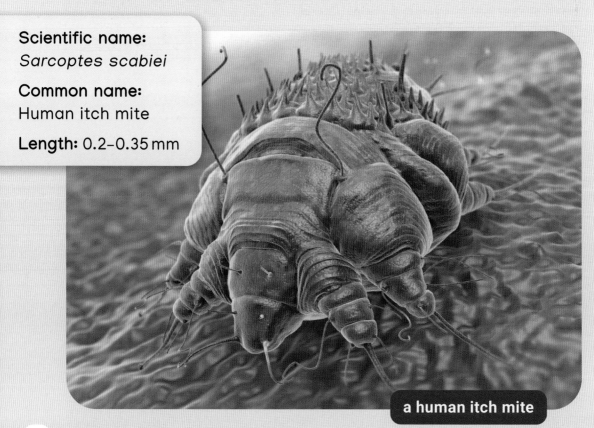

a human itch mite

Human itch mites can cause a skin condition called "scabies" — an itchy rash. This is the result of an **allergic reaction** to the mites.

Scabies can be treated with a special cream that kills human itch mites.

Putting cream on your skin can help to get rid of human itch mites.

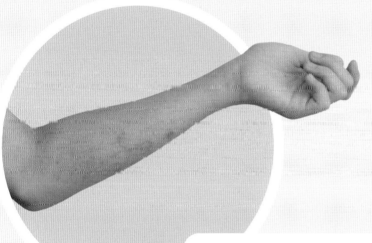

Scabies is an itchy rash on your skin, and looks like red dots.

Tiny Arachnids

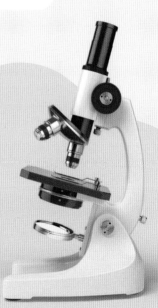

Like eyelash mites, human itch mites are arachnids. Without a microscope, human itch mites are hard to spot – they might look like tiny black dots on your skin!

Threadworms

Threadworms get their name from the fact that they look like tiny pieces of **thread**.

Threadworms live inside human **intestines**. But how do they get there? Well, if you get tiny threadworm eggs on your hands and touch your mouth, you might end up accidentally swallowing them!

Threadworms are long and thin, like thread.

Scientific name: *Enterobius vermicularis*

Common name: Threadworm

Length: About 2–13 mm

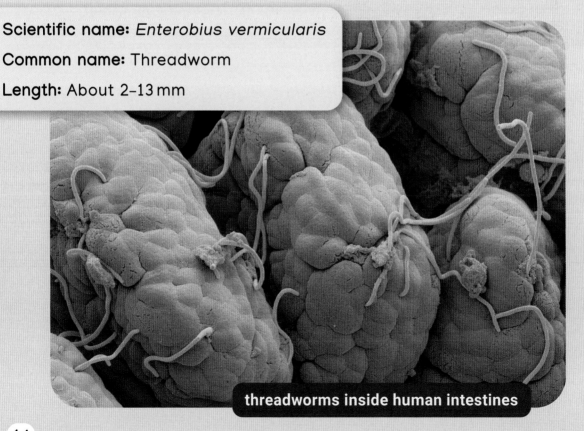

threadworms inside human intestines

The main problem with threadworms is that they can give you a really itchy bottom. They sound gross, but don't worry — they are harmless. Threadworms are quite common, but they are easy to get rid of with a chewable tablet, which can taste like chocolate!

Taking a tablet is an easy way to get rid of threadworms if you have them.

More Worms

Other worms, like tapeworms, can also live inside humans, but they hardly ever do. Tapeworms are more common in pets instead.

Fungi

Fungi (say: *fun-gee*) grow from tiny **spores**, which attach themselves to other living things or things that used to be alive. Fungi grow well in warm, damp places.

There are lots of different types of fungi, including toadstools and mould. You won't find them on the human body, but there are other fungi that can grow on people.

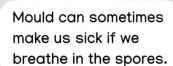

Mould can sometimes make us sick if we breathe in the spores.

Toadstools grow in the ground.

Most of the fungi that live on people are harmless. But there are some that can cause **fungal infections**.

Athlete's foot is a kind of fungal infection that occurs on your feet. It causes the skin between your toes or on the bottom of your foot to become red and itchy.

Athlete's foot and other types of skin fungi can be treated with special creams.

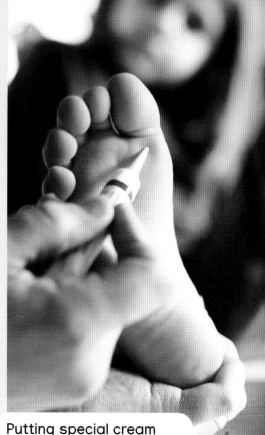

Putting special cream on your feet can help get rid of itchy athlete's foot.

Athlete's Foot

Athlete's foot gets its name because it's common among athletes. Sweat from exercise can create a warm, damp environment between your toes, and fungi are easily spread in places like change rooms.

Bacteria

Microscopic life forms called **bacteria** live everywhere, including on and inside the human body. Some bacteria help you stay healthy, whereas others can make you sick.

There are some types of bacteria that our bodies need, such as the bacteria in our **gut**. These bacteria help our bodies to break down food.

Some bacteria aren't harmful, but they aren't necessary, either – they are just there!

Good bacteria live in our gut and help us to not get sick.

Some types of bacteria can lead to infections that make you sick. Diseases like **cholera** are caused by harmful bacteria and can only be treated with a medicine that can kill the bacteria.

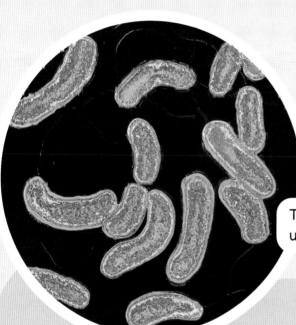

Harmful bacteria in our gut can sometimes make us feel uncomfortable.

This is what cholera looks like under a microscope.

Bacteria on Your Skin

Hundreds of harmless types of bacteria live in places like your belly button and your armpits.

Unwanted Visitors

There are a number of creatures that just visit human bodies, rather than living on them. Some, like mosquitoes, only stay for a few seconds. Others, such as **leeches**, can stay a bit longer.

Mosquitoes are small flying insects. Female mosquitoes feed on blood from humans and other animals. When a mosquito bites you, it spits, which causes an itchy red bump to form on your skin.

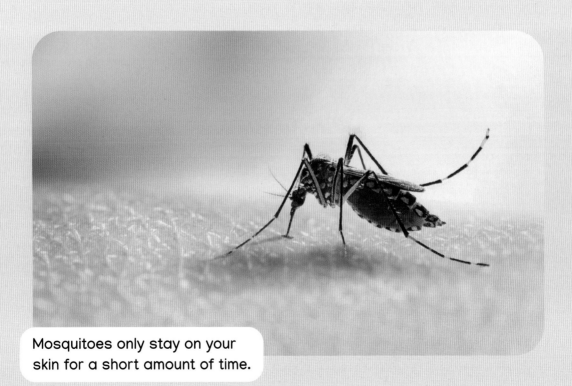

Mosquitoes only stay on your skin for a short amount of time.

Leeches are a type of worm. They attach themselves to the skin of humans and animals to feed on their blood. Depending on the size of the leech, they can feed for 20 minutes to over one hour.

There are different kinds of leeches, like the tiger leech, which has stripes on its body.

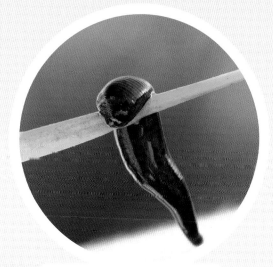

A leech can change size depending on when it last ate.

A leech can drink up to ten times its own weight in blood!

Living on You!

There are lots of tiny creatures living on you and other people, most of which we can't see. Although this may seem gross, most of these living things don't do us any harm. They are just there, so don't worry about them!

But some creatures can be annoying, and some can make you sick. When this happens, it's important to treat the problem right away and get rid of any unwanted visitors. Then you can go back to having fun!

Glossary

allergic reaction (*noun*)   a bad response in the body, such as itching

bacteria (*noun*)   tiny living things that sometimes cause disease

cells (*noun*)   the smallest parts that make up all living things

cholera (*noun*)   an illness caused by water infected with bad bacteria

fungal infections (*noun*)   diseases caused by fungi

gut (*noun*)   another name for intestines

habitat (*noun*)   the home of a plant, animal or other living thing

infestation (*noun*)   a large number of insects or animals in one place

intestines (*noun*)   the tube-like organ that extends from the stomach to the bottom

leeches (*noun*)   small worms that feed on blood

microscopic (*adjective*)   so small it can only be seen with a microscope

scalp (*noun*)   the skin covering the head

spores (*noun*)   small parts made by fungi that grow into new fungi

strands (*noun*)   thin pieces of something

thread (*noun*)   a long and thin string

Index